Fleet

A SECOND SELECTION

PERCY VICKERY

SUTTON PUBLISHING LIMITED

Sutton Publishing Limited
Phoenix Mill · Thrupp · Stroud
Gloucestershire · GL5 2BU

First published 2000

British Library Cataloguing in Publication Data
A catalogue record for this book is available from the
British Library.

ISBN 0-7509-2332-6

Typeset in 10.5/13.5 Photina.
Typesetting and origination by
Sutton Publishing Limited.
Printed and bound in England by
J.H. Haynes & Co. Ltd, Sparkford.

Crested china. Souvenirs like these were available in most towns and cities from the 1890s until the Second World War. They can be found in almost any shape with a local, county, regimental or personal coat of arms. A variety of manufacturers including Goss, Florentine, Grafton and Arcadian produced an amazing range. The origin of the three fir trees as Fleet's coat of arms is a mystery, and the earliest known local usage is in the Chamber of Trade *Journals* of the late 1920s, but much of the china is of an earlier period. The crests vary slightly between manufacturers. China representing the Calthorpe Arms, Elvetham and Ewshot is also known but no Crookham pieces are recorded.

CONTENTS

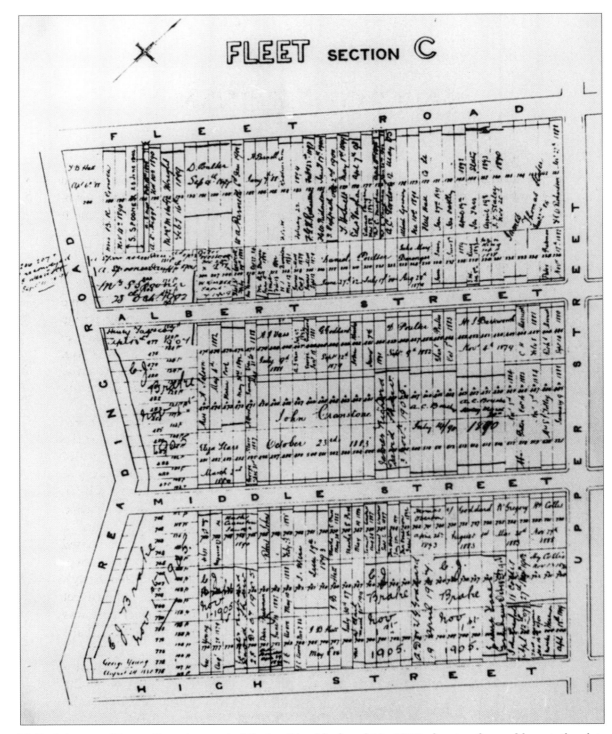

Mr Brake's map of the south-western end of the heathland he bought in 1878, showing the road layout, the plots and the names of those who had bought them.

INTRODUCTION

Fleet, originally in the Hundred of Crondall, was in the Tithing of Crookham and probably derived its name from the 130 acre pond at the north end of the town. The pond, the largest in Hampshire, was known in ancient times as Flete, and it was an important fishery in the medieval period. It became Crown property when the army came to Aldershot in 1854. The pond was designated a Nature Reserve in 1972 when it and the surrounding areas were bought by Fleet Council.

Merchants and travellers have crossed the heath that is now Fleet for hundreds of years. The Reading Road was part of the track between Farnham and Reading, while the Fleet Road connected Crookham Village to the mill and on to Hartford Bridge Flats. The siting of the Oatsheath inn at this 'busy' crossroads was no coincidence. With the coming of the London & South Western Railway to Fleet in 1847, the Station Hotel (later the Fleet Hotel and now the Links) was built and these were the only two public houses in Fleet until recently when four more sprang up at the top end of the Fleet Road.

The Whyte Lyon at Hartford Bridge (half a mile beyond Hartley Wintney) was Fleet's post office from the early 1700s until the railway came and took over the business from the stage-coaches. All letters originally had to be taken to and collected from the mail room at the coaching inn, where passengers would also join the stage-coach. Off-loading and loading was achieved in the three minutes it took to change the horses. In 1843 the London & South Western Railway Company reached Winchfield and was promptly given the franchise to carry the mails as it gave a faster and cheaper service. The main post office for the whole district was then based in a house in the station yard. Jessetts, at the lower end of Crookham Street, were appointed by the GPO to handle the local mail. By 1871 Windover and Dougherty's grocer's shop opposite the Oatsheath inn was Fleet's first post office. When Fleet Pond station (to the west of the railway bridge) was opened, the Fleet post was handled here as a sub-office of Winchfield, the mail being stamped with a 'Fleet Pond' post mark.

Fleet was granted Urban District status in 1904 and a council was elected with nine members representing the population of 2,000 and with a rate of 9d in the pound. With a growing population and the inclusion of Church Crookham, the number of councillors rose to fifteen in 1950. After the government reorganisation of local councils in 1974, the Hartley Wintney Rural District Council joined Fleet to form Hart District Council. Now the old Urban District area has twelve councillors.

By the end of the war in 1918 recreational pursuits in Fleet were varied, with football, rifle, golf and cricket clubs. Within a few years hockey, motor car and motor cycle clubs were started, and all attracted many members. Various hunts used Elvetham, Minley and Bramshill estates, as well as vast tracts of army ground. Fishing was permitted on the canal and pond. Tweseldown racecourse was the venue for three or four steeplechase meetings a year. Marching bands were popular and at various times you could join the Wesleyan, Drum and Fife, Salvation Army, Fleet Brass or Silver bands.

Traffic flow in Fleet was no problem in the first half of the last century except for the ten days in June when the Aldershot Tattoo was held at nearby Rushmoor Arena. Nearly half a million people came to watch the spectacle, arriving by car, charabanc and special trains. Up to forty double-decker buses were run by the Aldershot & District Traction Co. to meet each of the special trains that came from all over the country most nights. Hundreds of locals would line the Fleet and Kings Roads to see vehicles that we had only heard of. In those days Kings Road only saw the milkman, the baker, the coalman, and the regular 8A bus and about four cars daily, plus the occasional tank!

Church Crookham and Ewshot, south of the Aldershot Road, housed a few thousand soldiers in three barracks but the closure of Haig Lines in 1955, Leipzig Barracks in the 1960s and Queen Elizabeth Barracks in 2000 means that for the first time in a hundred years no troops are stationed in the area. The Gurkhas, who were loved by all the local residents, finally left for their new barracks at Sheerness in July 2000 – they had been based at Crookham from 1971.

Change in Fleet has not always been rapid and the work of the early photographers allows us to recreate a vivid history of the area beyond the immediate past. The photographers of the early postcards were rarely if ever named on the cards and it is only used cards that are dated. Many of the early cards were simply 'published' by a shop such as Radfords, Chorley, Bond and Crick, and the man behind the camera, often a local, received no credit. In the 1920s the name 'Roe' started to appear on postcards and photographs, and it could still be found on 1970s cards. They published thousands of photographs of the local area, revisiting the same places every five or six years.

Most of the photographs in this book are from the first half of the last century, while some are as recent as the 1970s. Some people may think it strange that these are 'old' but they record sights already lost to us.

1

Land & Water

Redfields House. Built by Mr Atty in 1879, the house occupies up to 20 acres in Redfields Lane. It has not altered much over the years and in a hundred years it has only changed hands four times. No doubt St Nicholas' School will be at the old house for many years to come.

Growing tobacco. In 1896 Mr Brandon bought or leased several fields in this area of Crookham where he grew cereals, hops and tobacco for many years. Tobacco was grown for several years on fields where the garden centre stands today. Note the original canvas-sided drying sheds. In other fields could be seen hops climbing 20 feet up their supports.

Drying tobacco leaves. By the 1930s the drying sheds had a stacking arrangement for the leaf-carrying frames to be hoisted from floor to roof. The sheds had slatted timber sides and earth floors to provide the correct conditions for drying and curing.

Harvesting the leaves. The leaves were cut and secured to drying frames to prevent bruising before being loaded on to the wagon. The average crop was 700/800lb per acre.

Bringing home the cows. Mr W. May had a dairy in Bowenhurst Road from 1910 till 1937. After milking in the morning he would take his cows along the Aldershot Road to the War Department field opposite the Wyverne where they grazed all day on the rifle range which was generally only used at weekends. Returning home on his tricycle he would then have to deliver the milk from a churn attached to his trike. In the evenings he would fetch the cows home and they stayed in the dairy until morning.

Hop picking. The whole of the area from Hartley Wintney down to Alton was planted with many acres of hops. In the late nineteenth century there were three breweries in Hartley Wintney and at least six in Farnham, plus the Crowley and Courage breweries in Alton all processing the local hops.

Whole families would turn up to help with the hop harvest. This family group was at Crookham in 1929. When the flowers were ready for picking they had to be gathered quickly as they would spoil if left in the sun or rain.

Hops were ready for harvesting in September and with Brandon's farm at Crookham, Howlings' at Cross Farm and Whites at Grove Farm – all with crops that required picking in a short period – there was always a shortage of workers. The Day Book at Crookham School on several occasions reports that 'many children were kept at home to help with the harvest'. This also applied when the corn and potatoes were gathered in.

Picking the hops started at daybreak when the dew kept the flowers large and open, and continued until about 9 a.m., by which time the atmosphere was drier and the flowers were closing up. Payment was made by volume and not by weight. The contents of the baskets were measured and then taken to the kiln. Once dried, then the hops were ready to be sold to a brewery. The kiln between Hitches Lane and the Green, now a listed building, is the last remaining example in the village.

Mr Edward Tudgey going fishing. His father Fred Tudgey opened a nursery in 1880 and later bought a piece of land in Pondtail Road and built another nursery there. This developed into a flourishing business which he sold in 1909; it subsequently moved to a larger site further along the road. He is seen here going fishing with his rods over his shoulder and equipment on his back.

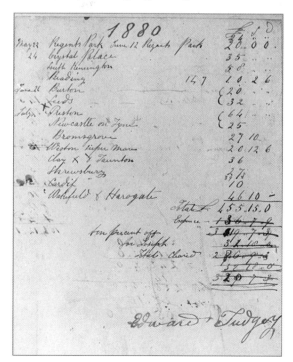

The receipt page for the first year's trading of Tudgey's Nurseries. Flowers and produce were evidently being sent all over the country.

By 1909 Mr Tudgey had decided to specialise in maidenhair ferns on a large scale and he bought several fields between what is now Crookham Road and the canal, close to the Fox and Hounds inn. He erected large heated glasshouses and was soon selling ferns to customers all over the country, mainly for table decoration. Other areas were set aside for flowers and vegetables. During the war lettuces and tomatoes were grown in the glasshouses and potatoes in the fields.

Mrs E. Tudgey checking the plants in the glasshouse. After fifty years of intensive cropping the soil was poor and the glasshouses were past their economic life so the nurseries were moved to Pilcot Road in Crookham Village in 1960. Here, the fifth generation Tudgey is still in business. The Crookham Road site was developed as the Sycamore Crescent and Fern Drive housing estate.

Ice-hockey team. A team of local lads in the 1920s ready to take on all comers. Even if their sticks were a disadvantage for ice-hockey, at least they could limp home with their support.

Ice-hockey, 1920. The pond froze over every year and annual ice-hockey tournaments were held here, with some teams coming from the London area. From 1847 special trains were arranged at weekends and evenings to bring skaters from London to the pond. From 1847 to 1869 the stop at Fleet was called Fleet Pond station.

Feeding the swans. When the pond froze over volunteers went out every day to ensure that no wildlife was trapped in the ice. They would break the ice so that the birds could drink and also provided food for the water birds.

Fleet Pond, often called the Lake. Up to the 1930s, it boasted a fine sandy beach at its eastern end which attracted dozens of families for picnics and swimming. No doubt the effect of draining the pond during the war allowed scrub to grow on the 'beach' and now only a small area of sand remains. The staging stretching out across the water is all that remains of the Royal Aircraft Factory's platform for launching early float-planes.

Fleet Pond and the surrounding area have been designated a 'Site of Special Scientific Interest' and over a thousand species of plants and animals have been identified in the 133 acres. The Pond Society and Hart District Council work together to maintain and improve the nature reserve.

Swimming pool and Fleet Pond. This was the view from the Up platform of Fleet station, looking towards Cove Road, from the 1930s to the 1960s. On the left is the swimming pool. Built behind a large new house in the mid-1930s, it remained open for thirty years. Houses now stand on this ground. In 1971, when the M3 was being built nearby, the owners of the whole of this view allowed contractors to dump thousands of tons of soil and gravel in the pond by the Cove Road before the Council noticed the illegal act. The night club/restaurant now stands on this site.

Gathering rushes. Poulters Bridge Cottage in the 1930s was a smallholding with various animals and a couple of fields. With the canal owner's blessing, the smallholder used to cut the rushes by the canal bank close to Poulters Bridge and his family would transport them home ready to thatch the hayricks.

When the canal burst its banks at Crookham in 1961 the canal bed drained for a long way on either side of the breach. Local youngsters often spent their spare time at the swing bridge opening and closing it for boats to pass, knowing that the boat-owners would tip them at least sixpence. After the breach the lads seized the opportunity to look in the mud for the coins that had fallen short – apparently several pounds worth were found and were shared among the boys.

The Howard family, 1916. The landlords of the Fox and Hounds inn close to the cemetery could always make a little extra by catering for the people using the canal at the back of the premises. Between 1916 and 1936 Mr and Mrs Howard ran a small fleet of boats for hire by the hour. Mr Howard's family is seen here in a couple of boats at the Fox and Hounds in 1916. Today's landlord organises a successful boat festival every year.

Canal regatta. For several years a carnival day on the canal has been part of Fleet Carnival Week. The earliest events were held soon after the canal had been dredged and restored. This is the 1992 event with the decorated boats pictured at Reading Road Wharf ready to set off to the Fox and Hounds. The return trip was made after dark with all the boats imaginatively illuminated.

2

Transport

Many of the local gentry had a horse-drawn vehicle in the early years of the twentieth century. Often the coachman would take the master to the station and then be available to take the lady wherever she was going. Here we see Mrs Waitham Long who lived in Adcote in 1905, almost opposite today's Vicarage in Branksomewood Road. The coachman is Mr Ian Moore, who lived in Victoria Road.

Bert Watts, milkman. The Watts brothers moved to Great (or Lower) Bramshot Farm before 1910 and built up a first-class dairy herd. Tom and Dick ran the farm while Bert delivered milk and dairy products around Fleet and Crookham with his trade bike. Two churns were secured in the front carrier and a third hung from the handlebars – he would have needed to make several trips a day back to the farm. The fourth brother, James, set up another milk-round with a horse-drawn float based in the Station (now Links) Hotel yard. Tom and Dick sold up in the mid-1920s but the two milk-rounds carried on through the war.

Mrs Emma Grit, chimney sweep. In the first half of the twentieth century most houses were heated by open fires burning coal, wood or peat, with chimneys taking the smoke up above roof level. The soot (a very fine oily powder) which stuck to the inside had to be swept out regularly to prevent fires. A 12-inch ring of hard bristles formed the brush head, which screwed into 5-foot-long flexible wooden rods and was pushed up and down the chimney, dislodging the soot, until the brush appeared out of the top of the chimney pot. This must have been very dirty and unhygienic employment. There were always eight to ten sweeps in the area but at sixpence per fireplace the rewards were good and steady. Mrs Emma Grit of Clarence Road was the only lady sweep recorded in Fleet and she is seen here chatting to Mr Harden outside his butcher's shop in the Fleet Road. Both started their businesses in the first few years of the twentieth century but Mrs Grit seems to have 'retired' after the First World War.

Lindfield's decorated van. Lindfield's ladies' and gents' outfitters were located by Lloyds Bank in the Fleet Road from 1936 to 1940. They decorated their 1937 9hp Singer Bantam van for the varied events in coronation year. They also boasted the 'Finest lending library' in town.

Vincent's decorated car. Vincent's the butchers had premises in Kings Road at the junction with Clarence Road. They decorated their car to show off their products at the various events between 1935 and 1939, such as royal celebrations and carnivals. Mr Vincent built the house, with shop attached, in 1906 and the family business survived until 1982.

Motor mower at the polo grounds. When the polo grounds first opened in 1925 the mower was pulled by horses but within a few years a motorised version appeared. An old Citroën car was stripped of its body and bonnet, its rear wheels were replaced by spiked metal wheels about 9 inches wide and a steel plate was fixed over the engine to keep the rain off. The blacksmith from Stevens' Garage in Fleet Road carried out the conversion. The vehicle was capable of pulling a triple set of mowers giving a cut 15 feet wide. It lasted until the club closed in 1939.

Golf club tractor. This was a Ford Model 'N' modified by Pattersons for working on golf courses. Pneumatic front tyres, wide steel rear wheels with short spikes for grip and a tipping body were the main features. The special sand in the bunkers had to be changed every year and topped up on a weekly basis. There were at least fifty bunkers on the course so the tractor was rarely idle, as the sand was stored by the car park of the North Hants Club in the 1930s.

Cane's delivery van. In the 1890s Mr Cane came to Fleet and bought Windover & Dougherty's small wooden lock-up shop and post office on the Oatsheaf corner. He employed three men to solicit orders from the 'big' houses and errand boys to quickly deliver the groceries and soon built up a noted business. By 1913 two delivery vehicles had replaced the errand boys to give a better service. This 15.6hp Wolseley CA van was one of the first grocery delivery vehicles in Fleet.

This 1926 11.9hp Morris Cowley 'Bullnose' was no doubt one of the first cars bought by Bradley Mathews and they obviously used it locally for publicity purposes. The advertisement proclaims '73 hour non-stop engine trial. Get our list of 30 other bargain used cars.' Their garage was modern in appearance, with an attractive office frontage. The two pumps and showrooms were in Fleet Road, almost opposite Stockton Avenue, with workshops behind going through to Albert Street. A paint spray shop was built, which in the 1950s was occupied by a DIY business. The garage closed at the onset of the Second World War.

Aldershot & District bus. The Aldershot & District Traction Co. was founded in 1906 with only one or two routes and it was not until Christmas 1912 that there was a service to Fleet. This service via Crookham cross-roads eventually became the No. 8 route and terminated at Fleet station, where this 40hp Daimler CC is shown. The conductress Elsie Ridgers must have been one of the first 'clippies' employed, and her family worked on the 'Traco' for many years. The company bought eight of these buses in 1913/14, five of which received new larger bodies in 1920/22: they were obviously very reliable.

Dennis charabanc. This may be one of Mr Lukey's later vehicles which regularly took club and public house outings to the coast, usually Bognor Regis or Southsea, in the 1930s. With the arrival of pneumatic tyres, passengers had a quicker and more comfortable ride.

Coach outing, 1930. In 1927 Mr Warren of Atbara Road bought a fleet of ten Guy buses and operated the Fleet Coaching Co. as well as running a Fleet to Aldershot bus service. Most of his vehicles were engaged in private hire. Here he is in 1930 picking up a club, possibly at the New Hall for a seaside outing.

A Red Cross outing. Fleet Coaches are seen here picking up the members for an outing organised by the Fleet Branch of the Red Cross. Regular trips were run by the Fleet Branch for many years for the elderly and infirm. Jack Rushbridge was the driver on this day.

Sunday School outing. For two or three years before the outbreak of war in 1939 the Methodist Sunday School Superintendent Charlie Perrin organised an annual outing to Bournemouth and Swanage by special train. The various Sunday Schools in Fleet would pay for the children to have a day out at the seaside – for many it was the only time they saw the sea. The train would be ten to twelve coaches long and could carry 800 or more. Any surplus seats would be offered to other children and their mums at a nominal fare. The train would leave about nine o'clock with its special headboard 'Fleet Sunday Schools'. On arrival at Swanage Mr Perrin would take all the children on to the beach and they would wait while he hoisted a banner that could be seen from all along the beach. At lunchtime he rang a large bell which was the signal for the children to come and get their sandwiches, cake and a cold drink. After the war the trips were revived and they continued well into the 1950s.

The Down platform, Fleet station. Fleet station was completed in 1904 when the tracks were increased from two to four. Passenger care was very important: a length of both platforms was covered to the edge and the footbridge was also covered. In the early 1920s W.H. Smith opened a bookstall adjacent to the access to the Down platform but it was forced to close in the late 1930s, probably because of staffing problems. These buildings were demolished in 1965 and a modern station – with no thought for customer comfort – was built on the same platforms.

Station Approach, Fleet, 1930s. The covered entrance where you could alight in the dry from your carriage or car can be seen just in front of the two taxis. The parcel shed is behind the waiting car and there are goods trucks on the right. The buffers stood where today you enter the car park road, just inside the station approach; there were also two or three tracks running up to the end of the car park by the pond.

Station Approach, Fleet, mid-1960s. By this time, just before electrification, the tracks in the goods yard were not used and nor was the parcels shed (on the far right). Parking areas were already being laid out – in the late 1950s and 1960s the number of commuters using the station increased rapidly, and most of them would drive to the station. Prior to the end of goods traffic no cars could be left at the station.

Wharf Cottage. An eighteenth-century cottage along the Crondall Road, just over Chequers Bridge, is believed to be the original canal wharfinger's office and home. Mark Hicks lived here from the 1920s until his death in 1966 at the age of ninety-two. Just across the canal by the bridge is Crookham Wharf, where all the coal, bricks, timber and so on which was carried by barge to and from Crookham was handled.

When the Crookham Brick & Tile Co. ceased trading at the turn of the twentieth century not all of their barges were immediately disposed of. No. 4, a wide boat, stayed here on the canal between Poulters Bridge and Chequers Bridge for several years waiting for a buyer.

Fremlin's van. In the 1920s this brewery van came to rest against the wall of the end house of Coronation Cottages on the Clarence Road and Upper Street junction. Over the years there have been hundreds of accidents, many of them serious, on the various crossroads in Fleet. We should perhaps blame Mr Brake, who laid out the road system in 1878 'in the American style', but I suppose he couldn't foresee the mass use of vehicles fitted with combustion engines.

Tank accident. After the war many soldiers were taught to drive tanks on the common around Church Crookham while they were stationed at Haig Lines. In 1947 REME at Arborfield kept their tanks at Martins Lines close to the North Horns (now Tweseldown). While learning to drive a 1947 Sherman tank with gun and turret removed on the road in 1953 one soldier got his controls wrong in Beacon Hill Road: accelerating over the pavement and across a garden, the tank embedded itself in Laurel Cottage. It took more than a week to shore up the house before the tank could be pulled out by a Scammel recovery vehicle. Before 1956 the house had been demolished.

In 1925 W. Davies & Son opened a garage in the premises that had previously been used by Thomas King bodybuilders for several years in the Fleet (now Crookham) Road between the two entrances to St James Road. There were two petrol pumps at the back of the pavement and cars used to park at the kerbside to fill up. On one occasion in about 1947 something went wrong and the car burst into flames when the engine started – luckily nobody was injured.

For several years a London coach used to bring air stewardesses from Heathrow to their homes in this area after their tour of duty, and collect others who were just starting their tour. On this occasion, as he was going along Fleet Road towards the station, the driver was taken ill and the coach veered across the road and came to rest embedded in the side of the shop. It was more than a week before the shop was shored up and the coach could be removed. Nobody else was hurt.

3

At Play

Crookham mummers. The mummers seem to be peculiar to north Hampshire. The performance involves six or seven men, some playing more than one part, telling a traditional story (some say it has been the same since Norman times) each Boxing Day. Three performances are given, with a collection for charity. Trim Tram, Bold Roamer, King George, the Turkish Knight Bold Slasher, Father Christmas and the Doctor are some of the principal roles, and their costumes are decorated with strips of coloured paper. Bramshill House had a troupe of mummers and in the 1930s they used to perform on Christmas Eve.

Fleet Silver Band. In the late 1920s Fleet could boast two bands – one silver, the other brass – and there was great rivalry between the two. A local businessman who was in the Brass Band provided a piece of ground where a hut was built for the band to practise in, but with the band's demise during the war the hall was used by a Slate Club and also the St John Ambulance Brigade. The band was resurrected after the war but finally laid down the baton in 1956. The St John Ambulance Brigade eventually bought the site and built their new headquarters there in 1982. By 1929 Mr Mill, the leader of the Silver Band, had his workshop in Upper Street and he allowed the band to practise in the workshop in the evenings. The Silver Band had become defunct in the 1960s, just before Mr Mill retired and moved away.

The Salvation Army Band. This band toured the town on Sunday mornings, singing hymns and saying a few words here and there, and hoping to pick up a few converts. They went down to Crookham Village every four to six weeks and would hold a service on the green outside Jessett's shop. On this occasion, in the early years of the 1900s, they were persuaded to pose outside the shop, possibly by George Jessett who was a keen photographer.

Red Diamond Band. Regular features of the New Halls' programme were whist drives and bridge, plus meetings of women's and men's groups. The floors of both halls were marked out for badminton courts and both modern and old-time dancing always attracted a good crowd, including many soldiers stationed locally. Most of the bands were local but a ball would attract a nationally known band. Groups like the local Red Diamonds shown here in 1923 consisted mainly of young people. The drummer here was Reg Karn, who lived in Fleet all his life.

School concert. In the 1930s Crookham School had several enthusiastic art and drama teachers and their annual show was always well received, according to a couple of parents (now great-grandparents) who are still living locally.

This was the school orchestra in 1937. They were coached by Mr Dodge, a senior master. All the children would have brought their own instruments. No doubt the orchestra played at assembly on special occasions and at shows at which the parents were present.

Army Cadet Force Band, *c.* 1942. During the war the Army Cadet Force and the Air Training Corps were formed and many boys joined the local units. The training given helped the boys when they were called up into the services. After the war National Servicemen were given six weeks' basic training but those with ACF/ATC training joined at week three, only four weeks before joining their units. Company Commander Captain Hodkin and 2nd Lieutenant Salter were the two leaders until the mid-1950s.

The Scout Association, comprising older scouts, formed a band to play in the carnival each year through the 1950s and early 1960s. Dennis Mallinson was the drum major and each year the band entertained the crowd with their music and antics.

Fleet Carnival Band, 1959. Alex Fitzpatrick is leading the band. The Suez crisis had ended just before the carnival, so the theme for this year was 'The 13th Suez Canal Lancers'. Themes in other years included 'St Trinian's All Girl Band' and 'The East Cheam Colonials', inspired by the film and the Tony Hancock character respectively. For several years they borrowed their instruments from the defunct Brass Band but the band's trustees sold off the instruments in 1966 and that finished the Carnival Band.

Country dancing. Before the war, when a large proportion of the world map was 'pink', all the schools celebrated Empire Day (24 May). In the 1960s political changes resulted in the day being renamed 'Commonwealth Day'. It was the only day when the whole school assembled, together with the governors and managers, and various tableaux were performed for the visitors. In 1925 three boys and three girls gave a country dancing display. Some of these children's families still live in the Fleet area today.

Another school play in the 1930s was *Don Quixote*. Many hours would have been spent making costumes and rehearsing before the show was fit to show to the parents. The cast seem very proud of their efforts at Crookham.

Girl Guides' pageant. The Crookham Girl Guides held a garden party at Mrs Wynne's house in Aldershot Road each year to raise funds and to show how much the girls had learnt. The afternoon ended with a pageant, which this year was entitled 'Cries of London'.

Dancing around the maypole, 1925. The maypole was set up at in the playground at Fleet School on several occasions for Empire Day celebrations.

Cinema staff. Fourteen staff ran the cinema in 1946/7. Mr Fricker was the manager and there were projectionists, usherettes and maintenance men; they also staffed the café next door. The programme was changed (generally) on Sundays, Mondays and Thursdays. The cinema was on the east side of Fleet Road, 100 yards up the road from Upper Street. The site today has one large and four smaller shops, with a layby. A lecture and concert hall was opened on this site in 1891 and it showed early silent films and soon became a full-time cinema. In its long history it had been rebuilt once and also enlarged, but it closed in 1957.

Fleet Players. This production of *Journey's End*, set in the trenches in the First World War, was produced in the spring of 1954 at the Institute in Albert Street. Dr Falkland Cary, a prolific playwright who wrote and collaborated in more than sixty plays, founded the Players soon after he came to Fleet in 1944.

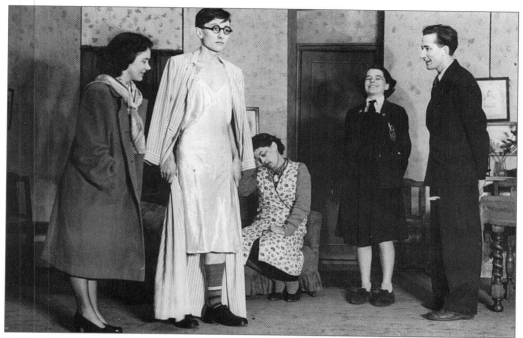

Fleet Players in a scene from the spring 1950 production *Bed of Roses* by Falkland Cary. The stage at the Institute was of a good size and the hall seated more than 200. From 1945 till 1971 all productions were staged here.

Fleet Players in *Night Must Fall* by Emlyn Williams, which was produced in November 1952. With the opening of the Assembly Hall (now the Harlington Centre) in 1972, all future productions were held in the modern hall. There were a few problems initially with the acoustics but they were later overcome.

Fleet Players won publicity by appearing in the Fleet Road on the Saturday before the show in their costumes, and selling tickets on the spot. These were advertising *The Bride and the Bachelor* in October 1959. Dr Falkland Cary died in 1989 and ten years later the curtain finally came down on the Fleet Players.

The Beverley Hillbillies. One entry in the 1964 Carnival processions featured the Clampits, a very popular American television comedy. Characters included Granny, Jed, Jethro and Ellie May. They were portrayed by the staff of Edna's, the ladies' hairdressers close to the old post office in the Fleet Road. The car looks rather grand and is obviously rare as it could not be identified by the National Motor Museum!

This is Mr Bowers' delivery van decorated for a carnival procession in the early 1950s. The Bowers family ran a grocery business for several years in Fleet Road from premises close to the old cinema site.

Firemen's float. For several years in the 1950s and 1960s Freddy Manfield and a couple of his firemen mates would hitch a trailer behind his car and with a bucket of water and a ladder would keep the carnival crowd amused and on their toes. Somehow they also managed to fill several collecting-boxes on the way!

Fleet Carnival Band. Some of the bandsmen used their own instruments but most borrowed them from the now defunct Brass Band. As well as taking part in the main procession, they would also parade with the children on the Saturday.

This is County Commercial Cars' entry in the carnival procession, with their own tractor towing the two trailers. The first had a drive mechanism which turned the carousel and made the horses go up and down; the second trailer carried the band and clowns. Between the 1950s and 1960s Stevens Garage, Technograph & Telegraph, and County Commercial each entered a tableau. They were always of a very high standard and by 1965, when Technograph moved to Bracknell, the honours of being the cup winners was about even in the commercial tableau class.

'Tulips from Amsterdam' was another carnival entry by County Commercial Cars, again with two trailers being towed by one of their tractors. The windmill blades were turned by the trailer wheels, and the scene was set off by a Dutch band and dancers. For several years these floats were also taken to Basingstoke Carnival but this stopped when the police started enforcing the Road Traffic Act.

'Ah Men' was the Reading Road Young Wives' entry in the 1962 carnival. There was always great rivalry between the various ladies groups, most of which in those days could boast about a hundred members each.

The 'MUM' Majorettes was the Fleet Mothers' Union entry in the 1973 carnival. The procession went along Albany Road and down Kings Road in those days, rather than taking today's route straight along Connaught Road.

Robin Hood was the All Saints' Wives' Group entry in the 1987 Children's Carnival and is shown here having just turned into Fleet Road from Kings Road. For many years the first Saturday of carnival week was children's day, with all the events in the afternoon being for them.

4

Religion

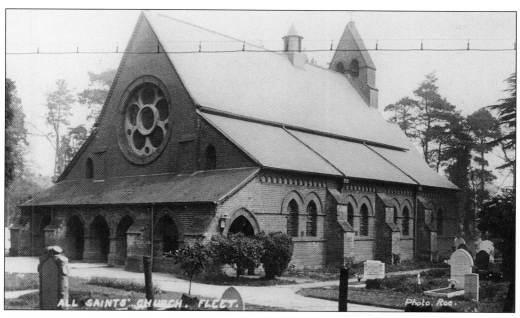

All Saints' Church. Mr Lefroy, the squire of Crondall (which included Fleet), laid the foundation stone in 1860 in memory of his wife Janet. The church was completed by Janet's father, as Mr Lefroy died a year before it was consecrated in 1862. The marble tomb with the recumbent figures of Mr and Mrs Lefroy now stands at the back of the church.

The Chester miracle cycle. This medieval religious drama was performed at Lobswood in Wood Lane in May 1954. This scene is part of the 'Last Judgement'. The drama was in two parts, performed on two evenings, and there were three complete performances spread over six days. Originally written by a monk of Chester Abbey in 1228, the plays were revived at Chester during the Festival of Britain in 1951 and repeated the following year. This production was only the third since the reign of Elizabeth I and was performed in medieval costume.

The trade card of Mr Parsons, wood and stone carver. Mr Parsons lived in Elms Road from the end of the First World War until the 1950s. In the 1920s he built a new house next door to his home – at this time there were eleven houses on this side of the road and only one on the other (Kings Road) side. Over the years he helped Mardles the stonemasons, especially in 1920 and 1921 when they were busy making the war memorials for Fleet, Elvetham, Ash, Crondall, Crookham and Hartley Wintney.

The first vicar of All Saints' was the Revd William Henry Plummer who was appointed in 1861 and served Fleet until his retirement in 1895. He was the longest-serving of the Fleet vicars.

Mrs Harriett Plummer, wife of the first vicar. Mr Plummer spent only a year in retirement, dying on 8 August 1896. His wife continued to live in Fleet until her death on 23 July 1908, aged ninety. They are both buried in the churchyard close to the chancel wall.

Fleet Roman Catholic Church. In the early 1900s services were held in a private house in Fleet, and the first church was built in 1908 on the corner of Connaught Road and Kings Road. By 1934 it had been enlarged, and again after the war, and by then it could seat 172. This building is now used as meeting-rooms and a hall. Pictured is the 326-seat church which was built by the side of the existing church in 1965.

Interior of SS Philip and James' Church, 1936. Built in 1900, construction was simple and cheap, with corrugated iron sheets fixed to the wooden frame, and wood panels on the inside. It was known as the 'Iron Church' or 'Tin Tabernacle'. After the Second World War there was obviously a need for a new church closer to Pondtail where the population was greatly increasing. Lobswood in Wood Lane was bought by the PCC in 1951 and it was here that the Chester miracle cycle was staged. Fernhurst in Kings Road was bought in 1957 and it was decided to sell Lobswood. The new church was built in Kings Road in 1966.

The Revd Pughe used to invite the parishioners to come to tea parties on his lawn on fine days. He was vicar from 1913 to 1916. In 1932 the vicarage in Branksomewood Road was bought and the Church Road site was sold. Renamed Glebe House, it was demolished in the 1960s and Glebe Court was built on the site.

All Saints' choir. This group includes Mr Pope the organist, Mr Prideaux the Albert Street School headmaster and Mr Edwards his deputy. Mr S.C. Mardles and two of his sons are also pictured on All Saints Day in 1901. Girls were not admitted to the choir until the 1950s.

Methodist Sunday School. Built in about 1908, the main building in Branksomewood Road behind the church had a stage at one end and could seat a hundred people. On the left was a smaller room with several sinks and ovens and plenty of tables; this room was hired by the Albert Street School for domestic science classes and every Monday morning the girls from the top two classes marched from the school for their lessons here as there were no facilities at the Fleet School.

The Revd J. Stuthard Mercer was the minister between 1922 and 1933, succeeding the minister appointed in 1914 when the Congregational church was built. In 1964 a Sunday School hall was built by the church and in 1999 planning permission was granted for radical alterations to be made to it. The Presbyterian Church of England and the Congregational Church united to become the United Reformed Church in 1972.

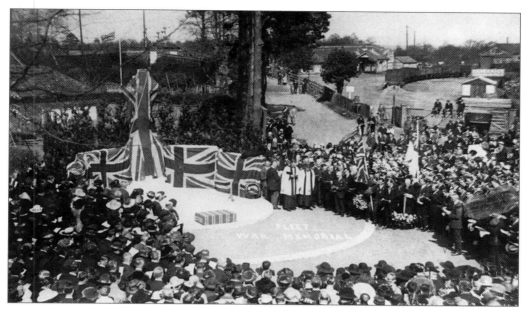

When the Cenotaph in Whitehall was unveiled in 1920 many towns decided to build their own memorial and Fleet was no exception. A site backing on to the Station (now Links) Hotel's bowling green was chosen and Mardles the local stonemasons were entrusted with the job. On 10 April 1921 the Earl of Selborne, MP for Fleet, unveiled the memorial, and the clergy of all the churches read prayers and the dedication.

Fleet war memorial. This photograph was taken on a normal working day soon after the unveiling: note the absence of traffic. The coal trucks can be seen in Station Approach, where cars are parked today. The memorial was moved to a site close to the library in the 1970s owing to the increased traffic flow and resulting noise during the Armistice Day service. It was moved to its present site in the car park when the new civic offices were built in 1986.

Christ Church, Crookham, was consecrated in 1841 by Bishop Sumner of Winchester for the parish of Crookham-cum-Ewshot and could seat four hundred. When the Guildford Diocese was created in 1927 Christ Church left the Winchester Diocese.

The interior of Christ Church. As happened in the 1840s and 1850s in some other churches in the south the congregation segregated itself here. The women sat on the south side and the men on the north, the girls near the harmonium by the vestry door and the boys beyond the pulpit.

Crookham Church. In 1841, when the church was dedicated, Anthony Lefroy was the first curate. In 1875 the Revd Gordon Wickham was appointed curate and when he left in 1883 his brother Wilfrid took his place as vicar, a position he held until 1925. In 1971 a meeting room and new vestry were added. The original building is connected to the extension by the south porch.

Crookham war memorial. Subscriptions poured in for this and a simple cross on a stone base was ordered from Mardles the Fleet stonemasons. It was erected close to the church at the junction of Gables Road and was dedicated on 10 October 1920. After the Second World War the base was altered to include the fallen of that war.

Elvetham Church. St Mary's stands in the grounds of Elvetham Hall but was closed for services in 1969. The church had been rebuilt in the Norman style in 1840 at a cost of £4,000, with traditional Hampshire flint facings. There had been a church on this site since 1250.

Elvetham war memorial. This memorial by the church close to Elvetham Hall was mainly paid for with estate money. The church became derelict many years ago and no Remembrance Day ceremony is held here. The memorial was unveiled by the Hon. Sir S. Arthur Gough-Calthorpe who was the Commander-in-Chief, Portsmouth, and the dedication was performed by the Bishop of Winchester. A thousand people attended the dedication ceremony on 22 April 1922. The names of fifteen village men lost in the First World War are inscribed on the base.

5

Industry & Health

Lismoyne Hotel in Church Road, opposite Lismoyne Close. The hotel was converted from a large house called Lismoyne which was built in the 1880s. It was one of several in the area built at the same time. The hotel opened in 1932. Extensions were carried out in 1970 when the catering area was enlarged and the function room and a block of bedrooms were added. Further alterations to the catering area were carried out a few years ago.

Bob Karn shoeing a horse in his blacksmith's shop in Connaught Road in 1909. Two of his sons, Joe and Reg, are with him. His house was called Jubilee Cottage but within a couple of years it was renamed The Forge. He lived here until 1935, but with the change of owner it had reverted to Jubilee Cottage within twelve months. When he first had the forge there were only three houses on the south side between Aldershot Road and Upper Street.

An early trade card for King & Barlett, a partnership that lasted about ten years. Tom King started the business in 1905 and with his partner he offered a very wide range of crafts. King & Bartlett and Stevens Brothers were among the first car repairers in Fleet. Their premises were in Fleet (now Crookham) Road, between the two entrances to St James Road.

Davies & Sons' garage. The company was founded by William Davies and his son, another William, and opened in these premises in 1935 in the Fleet (now Crookham) Road between the two entrances to St James Road. In 1947 the firm's first coach was bought. This picture shows the premises decorated for the coronation in 1937. The garage business closed in 1957.

The pumps and showrooms. The large showrooms were built opposite the original premises in the 1950s, and additional garages were built to house several coaches.

The paint shop, Stevens & Sons. In the 1930s the painters and signwriters here would have been kept busy painting the boards for farm and diary vehicles, as well as repairing cars perhaps after an accident, or in a new colour at the owner's whim. In the words of their brochure: 'A special feature of our work is our painting, lettering, etc., as we realise a high class finish proves a good advertisement for our clients and ourselves.'

The body building shop. Stevens & Sons, carpenters, were kept busy building dairy and farm vehicles, including hundreds for London's Express and United Dairies in the first half of the twentieth century. After the war a large batch of ex-army International lorries was reconditioned in the workshops to be used by British hauliers, as new vehicles were almost impossible to obtain. Then they started to build mobile library vehicles and there were always one or two in the workshop. These brought the Library Service to villages and outlying areas.

Stevens' Brothers' Garage. By the early 1950s the petrol pumps had been moved here, to what had been an empty piece of ground. During the war the site had housed a static water supply tank – about 6 feet high and 30 feet in diameter – which would enable fires to be put out even if the mains water supply had been cut. There was also a smoke room on the site. Stevens' Garage ran from the north entrance to the Hart Centre along the Fleet Road towards Church Road, and the whole site stretched through to Albert Street behind.

Rolls-Royce station wagon. In the late 1940s Stevens Brothers converted this pre-war car into a 'commercial vehicle' so that it would qualify for unrationed 'red' petrol – private cars could only use the 'white' rationed petrol. Several luxury vehicles were converted as there was no indication of when rationing would end. Here are some of the staff (left to right): Messrs Shorter, Chittenden, James, Legg, Skeates, White and Baldock, all long-serving workers.

County Commercial Cars' workshop. Founded at 127 Albert Street, here they had their workshop and drawing-office; across the road at no. 122 a couple of small offices were rented. In 1936, when Fleet Council vacated Ruby Cottage (no. 121), County moved their offices so they were all under the same roof but by 1955 they had bought the back of Claremont (nos 84/96) along the road and built new workshops and offices here. They gradually occupied the former Stevens' buildings (as pictured here) in the late 1960s. The white building on the right is the present car showroom and garage, but all the other buildings have made way for the Hart Centre and the car park entrance.

Tractors ready for shipment. By now the trading name was County Tractors and the despatch area was here at the Station Trading Estate. Generally, the 'cabbed' tractors were for the home market while those within (in the foreground) were for export. Note the heap of shale on the left: this was the residue from power stations which was used by the factory next door, Hemelite, to make breeze blocks for the building industry. They operated here from the 1950s to the 1980s, when they were taken over by Tarmac.

County Tractors always tried to supply a machine to meet the customer's needs and this was the result of one unusual enquiry. The customer wished to carry out seismic soundings for gas and oil exploration in the North Sea off the Dutch coast. Another order was received for machines to farm small islands off Tasmania. County took the opportunity to use the Sea Horse for publicity purposes and in July 1963 David Tapp crossed the English Channel in it from Cap Gris Nez to Kingsdown near Dover – and immediately set to work harrowing a field! The tractor floated at sea, and was propelled by the deep lugs on the soft-ground tyres as the wheels turned.

Technograph & Telegraph. This company's premises were on the corner of Albert Street and Upper Street and included the old Pool's furniture depository and yard, together with the Marsh Laundry site. T&T came to Fleet in 1954 and stayed until 1965 when they moved to larger premises in Bracknell. When the premises were vacated County Tractors moved in, and they stayed until 1983. Eventually the site was cleared to make way for the Hart Centre.

The print and inspection shop at T&T, pictured in the early days before the two-storey extension was built in Albert Street. The girls on the right are inspecting the finished products while the men are operating printing presses. The main product in the early days was a strain gauge, made by the etched foil process. It was made from a special resistant metal which reacted differently when subjected to strain either in compression or in tension modes.

The press shop at T&T. This is where the circuit board parts required to make the components were cut, punched and shaped. The company was originally called Techno Electronic Products and was started in a small production unit in the East End of London, where Dr Paul Fisler (who invented the etched foil techniques) evaluated the practical uses of their products. Eighty people worked at Fleet in 1965 before the company moved to Bracknell.

Huntley & Palmer, the biscuit-makers from Reading, had to increase production at the beginning of the war and this was achieved by turning over the whole factory to production with packaging being carried out by dozens of small workshops around Reading. There were two such places in this area. One was in Kenilworth Road on the corner with Avondale Road, where the Art Laundry stood before the war. Dae Health Laboratories moved in here in the late 1940s. The other place was in Sandy Lane in the building that formerly housed Warrens' buses. Here all the staff are enjoying themselves at their Christmas Party in the Institute in 1954 or 1955. As young men were called up for the services during the war, young women were 'called up' for essential domestic work to free up enough men.

Dae Health laboratories. Sited on the corner of Avondale Road and Kenilworth Road, the premises were built in the 1930s for the Art Laundry and after wartime service with Huntley & Palmer the Dae Health laboratories took over the front building. When they closed in the early 1960s houses were built on the site. Biscuits were still packed in the rear building until about 1956.

Albert Social Club. The club was founded in 1906 and made its home in the Albert Hall (later used by the British Legion) in Clarence Road, but in 1922, after internal problems, a new clubhouse was built on Mr Blacknell's paddock in Albert Street. Arthur Lunn was the first steward and served for many years. The club has had several extensions, the most ambitious being the two-storey function room and steward's flat added in 1963. The membership had reached eight hundred at one time. The club is still open.

The Broadway Club was founded before 1910 in first-floor premises at 4 The Broadway in Kings Road and moved to their present home in Albert Street, in premises behind 115 Albert Street that had been a builder's yard between 1930 and 1936. The building had a corrugated iron exterior with wood panels inside. By 1969 the changes in the gaming laws had allowed sufficient money to be raised to build a larger brick building for the four hundred members. In the last forty-five years there have been only two stewards, Harold Cox (a lifelong Fleet resident) and now Chris Powell.

A Hospital Sunday gathering on the green in Crookham Village, at the junction of Crookham Street, Crondall Road and Pilcot Road, 1909. This was the venue for most of the village events. Here the Salvation Army Band are playing for the hymns and the ornate banners are paraded – doubtless most of the village turned up to join in.

The Nurses Home was built in the early years of the twentieth century for nurses from London hospitals to convalesce after illness. While at the Home the nurses wore blue cloaks with matching bonnets. Eventually the Home moved to the south coast and the building, next to the Congregational (United Reform) Church, was sold. The house has now been demolished and an elderly residents' complex stands on the site.

Fleet Hospital was erected in 1897 after public subscriptions had raised £444; Lord Calthorpe gave the ground and £888. Over the years public subscriptions have raised the money to provide gas, electricity and the sewerage system. The eight-bed hospital increased in size and in 1948 it was taken over by the NHS. Over the last twenty years outpatient facilities have been added and its future seems secure.

Thurlston House. Situated at the top of Victoria Road, this very large house set in large grounds, was built in the 1890s. During the First World War the house was used as a Red Cross hospital for soldiers wounded in France, and some two dozen local women, domestics and VAD nurses tended the injured. After the war the house was returned to private ownership. The last owner was Col. Anson McCleverty who lived here from before the Second World War until 1960, when the building was tragically burnt down as the result of a workman supposedly setting fire to the roof. The council later bought the site and built houses and a block of flats for elderly people.

6

Groups & Parties

Fleet School opened in 1886. The block shown here fronted on to Albert Street. It was to accommodate 130 children. By 1910 the block fronting on to Church Road was built as the infants' school. The playground was fenced to ensure the boys did not mix with the girls or infants. The toilets were at the bottom of the playgrounds. When the church wanted to build this school, Mr Brake, who had bought most of the heathland that is now Fleet, sold eighteen plots (each 40 feet wide) at half cost. In 1947 the senior children moved to Heatherside School and in 1960 the juniors also transferred to Heatherside when the seniors had moved on to the new Courtmoor School. This photograph shows the infants celebrating the centenary of the Albert Street School. Not long afterwards the infants' school moved to the newly built Velmead School.

Fleet School, Standard 3, photographed in 1926 in the playground. There was a narrow concrete path against the wall of the infant school in this area but the main area was cindered.

Fleet School, Standard 3, 1931. These boys were ten years old. School photographs like these were very popular in the 1920s and 1930s, and it is not very often you see examples outside this period.

Fleet School, Standard 5. This photograph was taken in 1929, with the class posed in the girls' playground against the dividing railings. The fir trees close to the fence gave lovely shade on hot summer days.

Fleet School. These are the ten- and eleven-year-old pupils in 1947. Mr Fletcher (right) was the 'big' school's headmaster (his wife was headmistress of the infants' school) and he is pictured here with Mr Butler and his class. With forty-five pupils in the class, the imminent move to Heatherside School was certainly necessary. The move came in September that year and it allowed the juniors who were left to occupy all of the Albert Street block, with Henry Taylor as headmaster. It was only two or three years before the Fleet and Heatherside Schools were overcrowded because of the postwar population explosion. The corrugated building on the right is the canteen, which was built on the boys' playground and was often used as an emergency classroom.

Fleet School celebrated Empire Day with the Scouts and Guides wearing their uniforms and bearing the 'flags of all nations'. Here we see a 1930s parade getting ready to march around to the playground. The school governors would be present and the chairman would present the prizes to the top girl and boy and give a short speech. The children would then be given the rest of the day off. This was the only day when parents were welcome at the school.

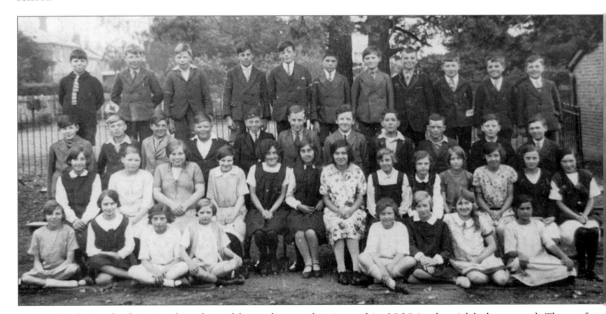

Fleet School, Standard 6. Another class of forty-plus pupils, pictured in 1929 in the girls' playground. The surface was loose cinders – very hard on hands and knees if you fell on it.

Fleet School, Standard 3, 1932. This photograph was also taken in the girls' playground with the outbuildings, including the cycle sheds and coke store, shown in the background. The coke fuelled the one 'slow but sure' stove in each classroom. At this time the classrooms were illuminated by two gas lamps hanging from the high ceiling.

Fleet School, Class 3, photographed in 1931 against the wall of their school in Church Road. These were the five-year-olds in their first year at school. For many years they were under the care of Miss Hawker.

A class at Crookham School pictured at their two-seater desks in the 1920s. Two children sat side by side at each desk, with individual hinged lids allowing access to their books and pencils inside. Fleet School had similar desks. At the back towards the right can be seen the chimney pipe from the 'slow but sure' coke fire which supplied the only heat in the room.

Crookham School. This is the top class of the junior school in 1959, pictured in the playground. These children would have gone on to Courtmoor School or a grammar school in the following September.

The 1st Crookham Girl Guides. This group photograph was taken in Mrs Wynne's garden in Crookham's Aldershot Road in about 1950. In those days they met in this area but today Fleet and Crookham guides share the Basingbourne Road headquarters.

The 1st Crookham Girl Guides on parade in the early 1940s on the clear sandy area between the Aldershot Road and Tweseldown racecourse. There was nowhere else for them to parade at that end of Aldershot Road.

The 1st Crookham Girl Guides parading along Aldershot Road past the saluting base in 1942 during the Crookham Warship Week parade. In previous years a War Weapons Week and a Spitfire Week had been held to raise extra money to help the war effort.

The Crookham Scouts approaching the saluting dais on the steps of the cinema in Fleet Road during the 1940 Spitfire Week parade. The idea of the various 'weeks' during the war was to encourage every body to buy 15 shilling Savings Certificates, thereby providing money which the government could use to buy planes and weapons. There would be a daily ceremony during the week when the 'indicator' (sited by the clock tower) would be adjusted to show the total collected.

Members of the Women's Land Army. During the Second World War young men had to register for the services when they reached their eighteenth birthday, so young girls were drafted into essential work at home. The Women's Land Army was the largest non-military group, with many volunteering to work in nurseries and farms. Tudgey's nurseries and the farms at Crookham and Crondall all had their share of WLA girls.

The Westover Road Victory party in 1945 was held in the Institute in Albert Street. Most people in Fleet, especially the children, enjoyed a party in their street with everyone contributing tables and chairs and making sandwiches and cakes in spite of the tight rationing. After five years of war everybody worked together.

Victory party, 1945. The Elms Road area was only sparsely populated in 1945 but the thirty houses brought out many children and teenagers to sit down to what must have been the best party most of them could remember.

On Coronation Day, 3 June 1953, many groups and streets organised tea parties after the main celebrations in London had finished. This party in Westover Road saw bunting hung up around the garden and tables laden with party food. The coronation brought a tremendous surge in sales of television sets and this was the first time people could see a coronation without moving from their armchairs, even if it was only in black and white.

7

Retail

Mr E. Hayes opened his shop in Fleet Road adjacent to Stevens' Garage in 1925 and stayed until 1935 when he moved into Reading Road South, six shops along from Tower House on the Oatsheaf crossroads. The shop is now run by the third generation of the family and is a specialist shoeshop and shoe repairers. In the 1920s the business advertised as 'Boot Maker – Repairs a Speciality' and 'Tobacconist'.

Walter John Edwards was born in 1870 and started working for Sydney Parsons, the butcher at Odiham, in 1896 doing a milk-round. Two years later he was sent to Hook station to collect his boss's brother Albert, who had just returned from Australia. They immediately became firm friends and in 1898 Albert opened his butcher's shop in the Fleet Road close to Church Road, with Walter working in the slaughterhouse behind the shop. At the onset of the Second World War the slaughterhouse became redundant but Walter worked in the shop until he retired in 1948. He moved to Connaught Road in 1925 and stayed there until his death in 1960. A lifelong Methodist, he joined the Royal Berkshire Regiment in 1915 and served in France where he was wounded and gassed.

Irving's Store. These premises, backing on to the canal at the top of The Lea, were built just after the First World War and comprised a house, shop and bakery. Mr Irving, pictured here with his Model 'T' Ford van, continued his business until just before the Second World War. The bakery business finally closed in the mid-1950s and the 'corner' shop suffered the same fate as most other corner shops, closing in the 1960s.

C. & E. Roe Ltd. This business was started by Mrs Florence Roe who lived in Aldershot Road in 1924 and continued by her husband Charles who built premises in Reading Road in 1927 opposite Albert Street. In 1962 he built a colour laboratory to the right of the shop. This was the only place for miles around capable of processing coloured prints and trade was good for several years until other premises were allowed to install this equipment. The car outside the shop is Mr Davies' American Studebaker, a very rare sight in Fleet in 1947.

The staff of C. & E. Roe, 1932. In the early 1930s quite a few staff were employed to run the shop and the print-processing. Included in this photograph are Charles Roe and his son and partner Edward (Ted), who wrote the book *Mainly about Fleet and Crookham*.

Woodman's Store, 4 September 1939. All the placards are declaring Hitler's defiance to our demands. John and Olga Woodman opened their grocery shop here in 1932. The premises had been built in 1896 as a double-fronted shop for Mr Raynor's hardware store. He also sold paraffin. Mr Wise later opened his pastrycook and confectionery business in the left-hand shop, but in 1946 both parts were under Woodman's name.

Woodman's Store. By 1950, with more and more houses being built in the Pondtail area, including Velmead Road, more floor-space was needed at the shop and a single-storey extension was added where an off-licence was opened. John and Olga Woodman retired in 1981 and today a butcher's shop and a supermarket occupy the site. The building has been a shop for 104 years.

Pondtail post office in Kings Road opposite Wood Lane. Owned by Mr Fowlie, it opened in 1905, when there were five collections daily from the wall post-box outside. Mr Fowlie was the sub-postmaster until 1936. This early picture shows the two outside gas-lamps which illuminated the window and the forecourt. This was a grocer's and greengrocer's nearly a hundred years ago and it is still a 'corner' shop serving a wide area and selling the same range of goods together with the post office facility.

Vincent's shop. On the corner of Kings Road and Clarence Road, this butcher's shop was built by Harold Vincent in 1906, together with living accommodation and stabling for a horse. He also bought an acre of ground in Pondtail Road where he raised chickens to provide eggs and fresh meat for the shop. The business continued to thrive in the hands of his two sons Leslie and Derek but it eventually closed in 1982.

Nelson and Goodrick opened their draper's store in 1903, selling a very wide range of goods with courtesy. If an item was not in stock, it would be quickly ordered. There were branches in Aldershot, Farnham and Farnborough, each managed by a member of the families. The business closed after the war owing to shortages in supplies; customers had only limited clothing coupons because of wartime rationing. In the 1960s the site was redeveloped as a modern three-storey office block, with shops on the ground floor, opposite Gurkha Square car park.

Fleet Market Place. When Oakley's (at the clock tower) was built this was the focal point of Fleet and the south side of the road to Reading Road was named Market Place, but the name did not catch on and by 1920 it had been forgotten and was never again mentioned in an address. Some properties had been built with balconies over the pavement, but nobody complained as the support posts on the edge of the pavement could be used to tether horses. Eventually the council had these extensions over the pavement removed. The building on the right is the Baptist church, in the days before it lost the 'front garden' to road widening.

A. & F. Bowers' shop. Between 1946 and 1961 the Bowers brothers had a grocer's shop in the Fleet Road nearly opposite Gurkha Square car park. On the right was a right of way to the slaughterhouse behind Harden's shop. On the left of Bowers' was a baker's with bakehouse behind. These premises have been a bakery since the First World War.

E.C. Boyes' small butcher's shop was one of several that sprang up at the end of the nineteenth century. This shop in Reading Road South stood near the Annes Way shops and only lasted a couple of years. At this period many farmers sent a horse and van to nearby towns to catch the local trade. Deliveries would be made to large houses and the meat that remained would be sold off cheaply to the locals. One Odiham farmer used to park at the Oatsheaf every day to sell his meat until he was banned.

F.G. Lanham's newsagent and tobacconist's shop in Fleet Road between the grey panelled shops and Church Road. There was a newsagent's on this site from the late 1880s until the mid-1990s. Beside Lanham's is Parson's the butcher's, and between Parson's and the corner stood Williams & Wright seedsmen and coal merchants. Their coal pens were to the side and back of the shop until 1960.

This was Cane's shop on the northern corner of the Oatsheaf crossroads until the family sold the shop in late 1950s. Within a short time it reopened as Holland & Barrett's groceries but with the major road-widening scheme at the crossroads in the mid-1960s the shop and the Baptist church next door were demolished and replaced by today's parade of shops with offices over.

Richard Pool's office on the right stood next to what is today the NatWest Bank. Richard Pool was a haulage contractor and furniture remover, and was the earliest horse-bus operator in the area. His business was founded in the late 1800s and survived within a few hundred yards of his office until the 1950s when it was taken over by Cantay's of Basingstoke. By the 1920s these houses with front gardens were gradually built along to Victoria Road, and then one by one a shop was built on to the front. Since the 1970s most of these have been demolished and rebuilt with a wider pavement.

W.H. Smith. This newspaper distributor had a franchise to have a newspaper stall at Southern Railway stations and space was provided at Fleet on the Down platform for a kiosk in 1926. After the war the platform offices were reorganised when British Rail took over and there was no room for the kiosk so a separate shop was built against the station railings. The station was rebuilt in 1966 when the track was electrified, but the shop was not rebuilt.

Grove Stores. Built about the time of the First World War, these premises in Reading Road South, close to Annes Way, are still trading today. Between 1933 and 1939 William Corderoy ran a general grocer's shop here, while next door Mr Clark had opened his hairdressing business in 'The Shop'. He stayed there until about 1970, and the shop is still a hairdresser's. In the 1950s the house to the left of the shop was called Silver Park and for several years Mr William Lunn ran a nightclub here. The site is now Silver Park Close, stretching back to Corringway. Several small shops were opened up along this stretch of the Reading Road but have since disappeared.

Acacia Café in Beacon Hill Road, late 1940s. Byrne's grocer's and newsagent's stood next door to the café on the corner of Aldershot Road. At the time the Molay family owned the café and Crossways garage was on the opposite corner. Note the WD stone with its broad arrow on the back edge of the pavement by the side of the shop: this indicates the military boundary. These stones were placed along the boundaries of the land that the army bought in the 1860s. Today many such stones can be seen around the pond and along the canal near Pondtail Bridge. The ground around the camps at Crookham were also marked.

8

Sport

The Stevens brothers entered the annual London to Brighton race several times with their 1904 De Dion. It is seen here in the 1930s at Marine Parade with Redvers Stevens driving and Syd Farr navigating. When it was not away at a show, this car was kept in a prominent place in the showroom at the garage.

After the war car and motor cycle events were very popular and they often took place on the vast tracts of army ground around Aldershot. One very popular sport was car rallying. Holland Birkett, the local vet and rally specialist, organised events for local touring car clubs which would cover the ground from the end of Pondtail Road to the tank test hills and beyond to Caesars Camp. Pictured here are Bill Davies and Jack Welch in a 10/15hp car trying to pass through an observed section without incurring penalty points.

In the early 1920s the Fleet Motor Cycle Club held meetings, navigation events and reliability runs, sometimes at night, with their small and less reliable engines. They are seen here outside the Oatsheaf, their usual meeting place, and to judge by their dress this is a social event.

Daniel Welch. With his father John at the top of his class at car racing it was no wonder that young Daniel showed interest and later an aptitude to follow in his footsteps. In 1997, driving a TONY Cart, he won the JICA class top formula for 13–16-year-olds. This season (2000) he is being sponsored in the Formula Vauxhall single-seater championship, and success could mean he turns professional next year.

John Welch in action. John's father was also successful competitively in both motor cycling and car events so it was no surprise that John was soon gaining national honours in his field. He is seen here at Brands Hatch leading Jonathan Palmer in 1988, on the track where he won the 1986 Grand Prix. During his career he was a factory driver for both Ford and Vauxhall and between 1969 and 1993 he was five times overall British rallycross champion.

Jack Welch. Except for the war years when there was no motor sport, Jack would undoubtedly have gone much further in scrambling (now called MotoCross) and as a trials bike rider. He is seen here competing in a trial on army land at Aldershot in the 1950s.

Within a couple of years after the end of the war scrambles were being organised on the army ground around Aldershot and here at Elvetham on Forestry Commission land every Sunday of the season. Races were usually over five or six laps and were for experts or novices on 250cc, 350cc or 500cc machines. This area is now called Elvetham Heath and within a few years it will all be built on. There was always a large following to watch the thrilling races, especially as there were usually several local riders.

Fleet Cricket Club. The club ground is in Reading Road North, about three hundred yards down the hill from the Oatsheaf Hotel. The ground was provided by Lord Calthorpe of Elvetham and opened in 1905. By 1910 two Saturday teams and a Wednesday team were playing regularly. Wednesday was half-day closing for the shops in Fleet before the war, so the Wednesday team comprised mainly shopworkers and proprietors. All matches were friendlies in those days. It was not until after the war that Sunday matches were played. This picture shows the players during a cricket week in the 1930s.

Fleet Cricket Club's Wednesday team, *c.* 1920. All home matches were played on the Reading Road ground which they shared with the Hockey Club from the early 1920s. Players shown include Messrs Wilmott, Hayes, Pemble, Buckingham, Harden and Ancell.

Ladies' Cricket Club. Mr Barnett farmed at Cross Farm in Crookham Street opposite Jessetts from 1928 till 1936, during which time he laid out a cricket pitch and his daughter soon established a ladies' cricket team. An empty barn was utilised as a changing room and for refreshments. Not all the matches were serious and here a team in fancy dress are having a good time. Matches were played regularly against teams from Farnham, Sherfield and Reading, and it was not long before a men's team was playing here as well. The ladies' team was known as the Barn Owls.

Fleet cricket team posing by the pavilion, 1920s. In a few years time the club will celebrate its centenary on the Reading Road ground. Previously, from about 1880, they had played in the grounds of Mr Bloore's house, The Beeches in Minley Road (now the North Hants Golf Club).

Crookham Rifle Club was founded in the first few years of the twentieth century on land opposite the Wyvern, by the (then) fire station. The ranges of 50, 100 and 200 yards disappeared during the Second World War, but the club reformed after the war using the ranges at Leipzig Barracks at Ewshot Camp. This shield was won by the club in 1920, when they used to hold regular club meetings.

Mr L.R. (Bob) Fenwick was a member of no. 5 platoon of the local Home Guard throughout the war and his experiences on the rifle range led him to join the City Rifle Club. In 1955 he won the most prestigious Queen's Prize at Bisley. A total of 1,254 competitors entered the three-day event. After firing 81 shots at distances between 200 and 1,000 yards, Bob scored 286 out of a possible 300 points, winning by one point. The Duke of Gloucester presented the prizes and Bob was ceremonially chaired by his friends and club members.

Fleet Football Club was founded in the late nineteenth century and in the early days they played at the bottom of the Views where Campbells Close is today, and later at Watsons field in Fleet Road by Birch Avenue. Lord Calthorpe gave them their present ground in Crookham Road and this photograph shows the team selected for the first match on their new ground on 3 March 1923.

Crookham Ramblers Football Club. C. Chillery, P. Savage, S. Coutts, M. Munday, F. Dudley, E. Townsend, K. Gardner, L. Galaher, P. Upwood, C. Stephens, R. Byrne, D. Oakes and mascot Les Galaher's son were in the squad for the 1959/60 season. The club was active between the 1950s and 1970s. Originally they played in Crookham Village behind the Social Club in a field lent by Mr White, but in later years they played on the Abercorn ground opposite the Wyvern inn.

Fleet Football Club. E. Wheatcroft, J. Brooks, D. Alner, R. Sawyer, J. Cook, R. Byrne, B. Gilbert, coach S. Brown, B. Stephens, J. Davidson, A. Piper and R. Silvester made up the team that played at Hartley Wintney in the 1956/7 season. Before 1961 the club played in various grades of the Aldershot and Basingstoke leagues.

Fleet Football Club. A. Wells (physio), D. Cram, J. Maitre, D. Wells, P. Paul, D. Alner, A. Bayliss, J. Brooks (Manager), B. Stephens, T. Nash, B. Arnold, L. Hardaway and J. Charlton made up the team for the first home match in Division 3 of the Hampshire League. Fleet won the league with 50 points (2 for a win) from 30 games, scoring more goals (113) than any other team in the three divisions.

Fleet School football team, 1929/30. Mr Salter coached and managed the school teams for many years. Facilities for sport at the school were very poor with only tarmac and cinder playgrounds. Pupils marched from the school to the Views in Victoria Road once a week for about an hour and a quarter and there was usually only time for a game of rounders, cricket or football – if it wasn't wet!

Fleet Football Club. R. Cox, A. Dance, M. Threlkeld, R. Thorner, P. Moss, S. Burton, R. Silvester, R. Driver, J. Godwin and D. Marley made up this minor league squad in about 1947. About this time Fleet Spurs Club was formed. They played at Oakley's Park, providing the chance for more players to play on Saturdays, but there were still only the two grounds in Fleet.

Fleet Hockey Club. Founded in 1925, they rented part of the cricket ground for their season (October to March) and from their earliest days there were ladies' and men's teams. Seventy-five years later the arrangements are just the same! This is a ladies' team ready for a home match in 1929.

Fleet School netball team. On games afternoons (once a week) the two top classes would walk from the Albert Street school to the Views Meadow to enable the girls to play rounders or netball in the top field while the boys played cricket or football in the lower field (if it wasn't wet). On Saturday mornings the girls' and boys' teams that were playing in the Aldershot and Farnborough leagues would have to travel several miles to matches. This is the 1933 netball team with their teacher.

Ladies' tug-of-war at a summer fête in about 1919. The venue is not known but the ladies' intentions seem very clear, despite what the Revd Henry Robins might say! In later years the fête was held in the grounds of the vicarage (Glebe House) and later in the grounds of the adjoining new vicarage.

Fleet War Weapons Week in 1941 was the first occasion that the Fleet Civil Defence tug-of-war team competed – in their overalls. By the following year, when the Warship Week sports day in the 'council field' came around, the 'Civil Defence' team, with more training, new jerseys and shorts, proved superior even to the RAMC team.

Tug-of-war club team with their trophy after winning the Victory Sports in the Views. By this time the war was over and the Civil Defence team was being disbanded, becoming Fleet instead, and in the next year they entered the AAA Championships at the White City. The club was still competing well into the 1950s.

Members of Fleet Social Bowling Club pictured in 1942 with a fine array of cups and a shield. The club was founded in 1914 in premises behind the Fleet Social Club in Clarence Road. The Social and Bowling Clubs are both still very active today. There is also Fleet United Bowling Club, situated by the police station in Crookham Road – this opened in 1923 and is still thriving today.

The Fleet Cycle Speedway team pictured in 1954 before setting off for an away match. They rode against teams from a wide area and travelled in comfort in one of Davies' coaches (later known as Fleet Coaches).

Fleet Cycle Speedway track. This picture was taken during the inaugural match in 1952, which was televised by BBC South, when Stoughton Greyhounds were entertained by the Falcons. The ground, a disused hard tennis court, was rented from the council and the riders (and their parents!) cleaned up the ground and built the track, including the banking for the spectators.

9

In Uniform

The army incinerator was built soon after Aldershot Camp was established in 1855. The incinerator, with its 60-foot-tall chimney, stood not far from Norris Bridge, where the NGTE was later built. There was a constant stream of horse-drawn wagons full of rubbish from Aldershot Camp up to the start of the twentieth century when rubbish began to be disposed of elsewhere, and the chimney was subsequently leased to the RAE who mounted wind and temperature instruments on the top. When the RAE had no further use for it it was demolished in 1930. This photograph was taken by Mr Roe of Fleet, and shows Movietone News filming the demolition from the roof of a van.

Lord Roberts Camp Home. This building provided relaxation in the evenings for soldiers stationed in Tweseldown Camp (later Haig Lines) in the First World War. Constructed of corrugated asbestos and interior wood panels, it was built close to and almost parallel to Tweseldown Road but in the early 1930s it closed for a time while it was converted into a cinema showing silent films. By the mid-1930s it was 'now 100% all talking'. It was an army cinema but was open to the public, and it closed in the 1950s.

The Church Army Room, Crookham, was also opened in the First World War and provided recreation rooms for soldiers in the Haig Lines. It included rooms where dominoes, cards and darts could be played and there were also reading and writing rooms.

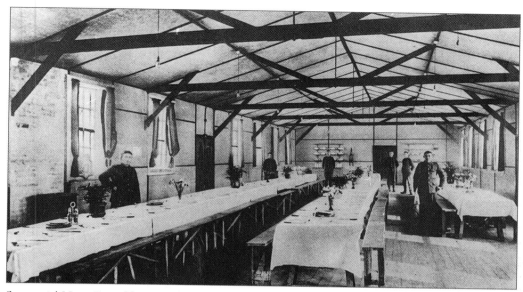

Sergeants' Mess. Tweseldown Camp (later Haig Lines) was a hutted camp at Crookham crossroads. In 1915 the RAMC moved in and the camp became their depot, and remained so until 1932 when they moved to Keogh Barracks at Mychett. The sergeants' mess was different to the men's mess, in that it had tablecloths, curtains and mess staff.

Queen Elizabeth Barracks. Formerly Boyce Barracks, this camp was built in 1937 for the RASC for basic Militia training in Sandy Lane close to the Wyvern. At the outbreak of the war the RAMC was brought back from Mychett, which was now too small to train the thousands of medics necessary and it was only in 1966 that they moved back to Keogh Barracks. In 1948 Queen Elizabeth (the Queen Mother) as Colonel-in-Chief came to Crookham on the occasion of the Corps Golden Jubilee and in her honour the camp was renamed Queen Elizabeth Barracks. The Gurkhas came to the barracks in 1971 but have recently moved to Kent, leaving the last wooden hutted camp in the country to the developers.

Territorial Army. 'E' Company, 4th Battalion Hampshire Regiment, comprised sections from Yateley, Farnborough, Aldershot, Odiham and Fleet. Company headquarters were at Redan Hill in Aldershot and this photograph was taken at Aldershot.

Territorial Army. This is the Fleet section of 'C' Company, 4th Battalion Hampshire Regiment, in 1916/18. They met in the gymnasium behind the Institute in Albert Street (now Richmond Court flats). Meetings were held twice a week and some time was spent at Aldershot. The Terriers were formed in 1908 and the men were partially trained before entering the army.

No. 1 Platoon, 'C' Company, Home Guard, of the 25th Battalion of the Hampshire Regiment, covered Fleet and Crookham. No. 1 Platoon usually met at the British Legion Hall where there was a large hall upstairs. Training took up at least one evening and Sunday each week, and more if there was any enemy air activity that week. When the siren sounded to warn of approaching enemy aircraft, everyone would parade to positions at strategic locations – at one stage in the war they were on duty every night for several months. Many nights were spent guarding the railway line and other important features from enemy parachutists and incendiary bombs.

No. 3 Platoon, Home Guard, was comprised mainly of Crookham men. They met at Dogmersfield House. As soon as the siren sounded they would be deployed in small groups watching out for enemy parachutists. No. 2 Platoon was entrusted with the spigot mortar while No. 5 Platoon had a Smith gun, which was towed behind Mr E. Tapp's car, painted khaki for the duration of the war. No ammunition was ever supplied for this weapon but 'Dad's Army' fired onions from their Smith Gun.

Home Guard officers and NCO's. No. 3 Platoon did most of their training in the 1,700 acres of the Dogmersfield estate which included woodland as well as grassland. During the war there was a defence line running across the area with obstructions along the canal between Winchfield and Crookham and across the fields to Pale Lane, where the River Hart was dug out wide and deep and defences built up to protect the nearby railway line, making it difficult to cross.

A Sunday morning route march for No. 3 Platoon, Home Guard. Initially this was no joke for a fifty-plus man who sat at a desk all week, only to find that on a Sunday morning he was expected to march 5 miles in heavy boots, wearing a thick rough uniform and carrying a heavy rifle on his shoulder. Younger people who today laugh at 'Dad's Army' are not aware that during the war a lot of what happened really was just as funny – unless it was you who fell in the muddy ditch early on a frosty evening.

In 1941 there was a Civil Defence parade and inspection on the barrack square at Crookham, when all sections of the ARP (Air Raid Precautions) were assembled in their 'action clothes' with their support vehicles. Here a section of the decontamination squad (gas dispersal) parades in front of Mr Crumplin's lorry, which had been commandeered for ARP use. On the door of the lorry the address still says Rose Farm but 'Fleet' has been painted out – it was the same on shop fronts. In addition, direction signs at road junctions and street names were all removed and if you were in a strange town you would have no idea where you were – but more importantly nor would the enemy if they managed to invade.

This is the First Aid section of the Civil Defence Rescue Squad at the same parade. They had a large fleet of heavier support vehicles. They were based at Pools, close to the station. The Auxiliary Fire Service was attached to the National Fire Service. Not all their vehicles were fire engines but they all towed a water-pump.

Fleet fire brigade. In 1920 Fleet Urban District Council replaced the pony and trap and cycling firemen with this Model 'T' Ford which would carry the equipment and the men to a fire much more quickly. In 1934 a Dennis fire engine was bought and this was the vehicle the crew took into the war and the National Fire Service.

Fleet's first fire brigade was formed in 1900 and they have had various vehicles, from the pony and trap (for hoses, etc.) and bicycles to today's sophisticated powerful engine and pump. During this time Fleet had had only four stations. This picture from the mid-1950s shows Messrs Harrison, Manfield, Ellis, Wright, Tarrant, Smith, Baker, Sub-officer Shorter, Burgess and Woolley.

Building the bonfire. For many years after the war until the mid-1960s Mr Harden allowed his field at the Firs Meadow to be used by the Fleet firemen to have a bonfire party with a giant bonfire and the best firework display for miles around in aid of firemen's charities. The rubbish for the bonfire was collected by many helpers over several weekends and the size of the finished pile can be judged by the picture. Firs Meadow was large and ideal for the many fun days including fairs, carnivals and gymkhanas held there. Mr Harden sold the Firs Meadow to Hampshire County Council in 1966 and the police station now stands on the site.

Church Crookham held a carnival during the 1930s, and here the fire engine is leading the other floats along Sandy Lane back to Crookham House, next to the church, where the procession had assembled. Crookham had its own fire engine from the early years of the twentieth century until after the Second World War but now Fleet station covers the Crookham area.

Blackbushe Airport. Hartford Bridge Flats was a 4 mile expanse of flat scrubland on either side of the A30 between Blackwater and Hartford Bridge – or at least it was until 1941 when the Air Ministry found it and decided to build an RAF airfield on the high plateau. The standard 1940 three-runway airfield was adopted with the main runway running almost parallel to the A30 and the other two crossing the A30 at an angle. RAF Hartfordbridge was actually established with the A30 still running through the middle! Soon, to avoid confusion, the name was changed to RAF Blackbushe, after the farm that backed on to the Forestry Commission land which hid the stock of bombs.

Handley Page Hermes IV. In 1946 the military aircraft moved out of Blackbushe and the late 1940s saw the arrival of Britavia, Airwork and Silver City air lines operating charter flights with Lancastrians, DC3s and Bristol Freighters. Here is a Britavia Hermes IV. Below its nose are the Silver City/Britavia radio and instruments workshops, while the distant buildings under its tail are Airwork's hangars. In the 1950s its official designation was 'London Airport, Blackbushe'. By 1955 there were 36,000 aircraft movements each year but with the opening of Gatwick the passenger business left Blackbushe and in 1960 it closed. Today Blackbushe is home to the Car Auctions who own the whole site, as well as a Sunday Market and a private flying club.

Douglas Boston IIIA. During the war many nationalities flew from Blackbushe, including Free French, Dutch, Canadians and Americans, as well as the RAF. This Boston is from 342 Lorraine Squadron which had evidently completed seven operations, as there are seven bombs painted on the fuselage. One of the four 500lb bombs carries a painted message which includes the word 'Hitler' – it all helped morale. The bombs arrived mainly at Fleet station and they were usually taken up to Blackbushe on 'Queen Mary' trailers at weekends – manoeuvring round the hairpin bend out of the station yard to get over the bridge took a lot of skill.

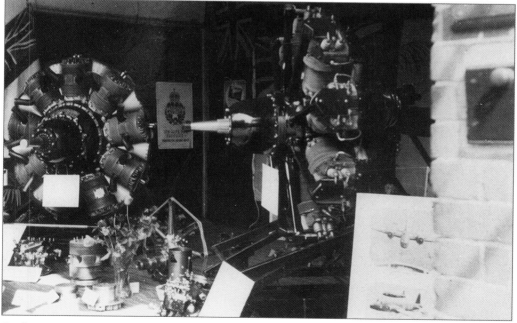

Spitfire engine. During Spitfire Week in Fleet in 1940, there were displays in various shops in the Fleet Road. The gas and electric showroom on the corner with Birch Avenue set up window displays pertaining to the RAF to encourage the public. At the other end of the Fleet Road, close to today's police station, Mr Davies also put on a display in his showroom. It includes two aircraft engines, one from a Spitfire, as well as various other pieces of aircraft.

Towing the spigot mortar. This weapon was obviously designed to be used by the services who could pick it up and put it in the back of a lorry, but as the Home Guard only had a car the weapon was unusable. No. 1 Platoon overcame the problem by designing and fitting a carriage to enable it to be towed by Mr Davies' car. As can be seen the wheels were detachable to enable it to be fired with its legs in the correct position.

The spigot mortar could be assembled on the base which has been preserved and will be resited in a suitable place on Elvetham Heath. The mortar was never fired from this base owing to the close proximity of the railway and the roads. A few practice firings were carried out at Dogmersfield Park using the method shown here. No. 1 Platoon with the spigot mortar were luckier than no. 5 Platoon with their Smith Gun, as they never received any ammunition.

10

Houses & Roads

The Holt. This large house was built for Dr Frere in the early years of the last century, and he lived there until his death just after the war. It stood in the Fleet Road midway between Birch Avenue and Westminster Close, on the opposite side of the road. An office block stands on the site today. Dr Frere was a much-respected doctor who in later years held his surgery in his home. He was a great benefactor to the people of Fleet, and was involved with many organisations including the hospital.

Minley Road, looking up to the Station Bridge in about 1905 – at about the time when gas streetlights were introduced in Fleet. By this time most of the houses in this stretch of road had been built, and only three more were to be added. Just after 1980 the road junction on the left was closed as a new road and roundabouts had been built a few yards along the road.

These two wooden houses were built in Cove Road at the start of the 1900s when building restrictions were almost non-existent. The main timbers and the cladding were untreated softwood and by the time they were demolished in the late 1960s there were doubtless some structural problems. A pair of bungalows occupies the site today.

This wooden bungalow stood on the north side of Clarence Road close to Reading Road, and was built when the road was known as Middle Street in the last few years of the nineteenth century. It was not demolished until another bungalow had been built in the orchard on the left in the late 1940s. The wooden dwelling was then demolished and a brick bungalow was built on this site as well.

Great Bramshot Farmhouse, situated in the Cove Road close to Bramshot Bridge, was owned by the Watts family for almost all of the twentieth century. From the 1920s Rose Farm Dairy was run by farmer Mr Adams and dairyman Mr Cubby but when Mr Adams was killed in 1946 Mr Watts went into partnership with Mr Cubby. This arrangement continued until Mr Cubby retired, but Mr Watts continued to run the dairy until its demise in 1999. Milk production ceased on the farm in 1947.

The Oatsheaf crossroads, Crookham Road, with the hotel which was built in the 1850s on the right. The horse-trough provided drinking water for the many horses that would have passed through this area daily. The parade of shops along the Crookham Road is still much the same today. The crossroads have existed for hundreds of years: one arm, the Reading Road, was the main road from Farnham to Reading, and the other arm was the track from Crookham to the mill and on to Yateley and Bagshot.

Mr Voller's bakery. This was one of the early shops in Fleet Road and it stood on the north-west corner with Church Road. It was an attractive-looking building hung with rich red tiles. Mr Voller opened his bakery in the 1890s and remained here until the row of shops on the north-east corner of the junction was built in the 1920s. The business finally closed at the outbreak of the Second World War. The village pump was behind Mr Voller's first shop – there was no piped water at this time. To the left of this shop stood a fine old cottage, also dating to about 1890, with a large front garden but at the turn of the century Mr Barnwell built a lock-up shop in the garden for his cycle business. The old house remained until the mid-1980s when the site was redeveloped with offices over shops.

Pondtail Garage. Sited between Aldershot Road and Kings Road, this garage was opened in the late 1920s. The direction sign on the right gives a name that was commonly used at this time, although Hartley Row is now referred to as Wintney, the name for the whole area.

In 1924 Fleet UDC decided to build council houses to be let to deserving families. These six were built on the corner of Kings Road and Albany Road, and another three pairs were built in Elvetham Road. The houses pictured were demolished in 1970 and replaced by Albany Court, a complex for elderly people.

Boone Farmhouse was situated in the Crookham Road, just past the police station. Now called Stanton Lodge, it was one of the original farmhouses in Fleet. The farm covered the area of the Lea. Even in the 1950s you only had to walk just past the football ground to see cows, sheep and pigs. In 1888 Sir Arthur Sullivan rented this house while he wrote the music for the *Yeoman of the Guard.*

The first Fleet school, near All Saints'. In 1860 Fleet had a population of 300, about 30 or 40 of them being children. Mr Lefroy decided to buy a pair of newly built but unfinished cottages, which could be finished inside as required for the new school. Within five years the need for larger premises became obvious and the school in Albert Street was built. The first school was then converted to a house and is still occupied today.

Silver Jubilee decorations in Fleet Road in 1935, viewed from the Upper Street/Victoria Road junction looking towards the station. A block of shops and two floors of offices replaced the garden and notice-board in the 1960s.

Dinorben House had extensive grounds with some 119 acres between Reading Road and Coxheath Road bridges. The main lodge in Dinorben Avenue still stands and there was also a service lodge in Coxheath Road. The latter was demolished when Wickham Road was built. The last residents of the estate were the Chinnocks and the Gallsworthys, who lived there from 1872 till 1935 when the estate was sold off in lots. This picture shows the service lodge with Mr Hewitt the gamekeeper and his wife. His duties included looking after the game and taking care of the vermin as well as general duties. Just along the road stood the service lodge for Courtmoor House.

Reading Road bridge. The second bridge at this site had a hump-back, but after the war it was decided to build a new, realigned, bridge without a hump. After much furore the boating fraternity lost their case for more headroom and the County Council got their humpless bridge. Today boats have only about 5 feet 6 inches (water) headroom and pedestrians have to bend almost double to get under it!

Ferndale Road. At the end of the Second World War there was a desperate need for more houses, and one of the sites selected was the area of sandy scrubland bounded by the canal, Coxheath Road, Gally Hill Road, Aldershot Road and Reading Road. This was one of the first private developments leading from Gally Hill Road by the side of Crookham School through to the Verne where it joins Award Road. The landscape has changed greatly with nearly fifty years of shrub and tree growth.

Aldershot Road, Crookham, in the early 1920s. There were houses all the way from the crossroads to the War Department land, as well as a couple of shops, petrol pumps and two coal yards. A few yards behind the trees to the left was the clear sandy area where processions used to end during the war and fifty yards further on was Tweseldown racecourse, the army's steeplechase course. The flat course was on the Queen's Parade Ground at Aldershot.

William and Frank Jessett outside their shop in the 1930s, with their house on the left and the bakery, store and garages to the right. The store opened in the 1830s and when the railway came to Winchfield in 1843 mail was carried by rail instead of by road and a post office was established outside the station. Once the mail had been sorted it was quickly sent over to Jessett's, who ran the Crookham post office. The store was the only one for miles and it stocked food, clothes, hardware and much more. George Jessett took many photographs over the years of the various meetings on the green from the balcony above the shop.

Dogmersfield House was built on the site of one of the palaces belonging to the Bishops of Bath and Wells. Henry VI often stayed here and Catherine of Aragon met Henry VII and her future husband Prince Arthur here. An Elizabethan house is incorporated in the eighteenth-century mansion, and it was the Mildmays' home for many years.

Dogmersfield House had vast gardens, including this large eighteenth-century walled garden close by the house and stables. On either side of the entrance are two dovecotes: one is said to be the oldest in Hampshire and the other the most recent. The garden today is much the same as in this 1920s picture except that the feature at the end has been removed. About 300 yards in front of the house is a 20-acre lake with an abundance of water-birds.

Dogmersfield Church. The estate workers' houses and the church stood between the house and the lake but in 1800 Lady Mildmay wished to have a better view of the lake and so all the buildings were removed. The church was rebuilt in 1806 in what was eventually the farmyard close to the road and a few years ago the whole site was in ruins, but now all the buildings seem to have been restored. This photograph shows the present church near the Queens Head, which was built in 1842. The bell tower housed four bells which sadly remain silent today because of structural problems, and there are numerous memorials on the walls inside. A sixteenth-century memorial to Anne Sutton came from the original church, and there are several from the second church.

Lord Mildmay's funeral. This was typical of the ritual observed over hundreds of years by the family of the 'squire', who had his own private church and burial-ground. His coffin would be carried from house to church in the horse-drawn farm wagon with the mourners walking behind. This was the funeral of the 6th Baronet, Sir Henry St John Mildmay, who died on 14 April 1918. He was born on 28 April 1853, no doubt in Dogmersfield House. Presumably he would be laid to rest in the vault of the second church.

Elvetham estate. The entrance to the estate today is along the Fleet–Hartley Wintney Road and the Hall has been a conference centre for the last forty-five years. Queen Elizabeth I visited Elvetham in 1591 and planted an oak tree to commemorate her visit – it is now more than 30 feet in circumference. An avenue of Wellingtonias just under a mile long was planted and the gardens reclaimed from 1963, as an ongoing project. A church has stood in the grounds since 1250 and the present St Andrew's, the former parish church of Elvetham, was rebuilt in 1840 by the 3rd Lord Calthorpe. It closed for services in 1969.

Elvetham Hall. The first reference to a house on this site was dated 675 and the manor has been held by various families over the years. In 1535 Henry VIII was entertained here by John Seymour and later by his son Edward Seymour. The hall burnt down in 1849 and a white two-storeyed lodge was built on the site. This was added to in 1860 and developed into the present mansion by Lord Calthorpe. During the First World War it served as a hospital for wounded officers. The family lived in the house until after the Second World War. It was sold to ICI in 1953 and on to Lansing Bagnall in 1965. In the 1980s the managing director of Lansing Bagnall sold the Basingstoke factory to a German company, but kept the Hall.

Double Lodges, Minley Manor. This was one of several entrances to the manor, all of which had lodges. This one is on the Minley Road about half a mile from Fleet station. In the 1970s, when the nearby M3 was being constructed, the road passing the lodge was straightened and today the lodges are hardly visible from the new road. The lodges were built in the 1860s when the manor was rebuilt by the banker Raikes Currie. The manor itself is a slightly smaller version of the Château De Blois on the Loire. One of the main features of the estate is the 500 yard avenue of Wellingtonia and lime trees. The estate, some 2,500 acres, was purchased by the War Office in 1936 as a training area and is today used by the Royal Engineers.

The stable block at The Lea. The house, which later became Crookham House, was of sufficient size and importance to have a fine stable block at the rear. In 1861 Mr Lefroy built the house next to Crookham Church, opposite the Wyvern inn. After the war it was sold to North Hants Properties, who converted it into Crookham House Residential Hotel. It was demolished in the 1960s to make way for a housing estate.

ACKNOWLEDGEMENTS

I would like to thank the following individuals and organisations without whose assistance this book would not have been possible: Aldershot Military Museum, Mrs J. Aldridge, Mrs C. Ashcroft, Mrs A. Baldock, G. Barson, Mrs E. Beale, Mrs E. Bell, W. Boulter, Mrs J. Bowers, Mrs B. Brown, D. Brown, Mrs F. Butler, R. Byrne, J.P.B. Coles, Mrs G. Cousins, F. Crumplin, Mrs M. Fenwick, A. Fitzpatrick, Fleet & District Carnival Assoc., Mrs B. Fury, B. Gale, D. Gardner, Mrs J. Grace, Mrs D. Green, Mrs R. Hardy, R. Harrison, D. Hayes, Mrs C. Heathers, Mrs J. Hedger, I. Hester, S. Jones, R. Karn, Mrs J. Mardles, Mrs B. May, D. Millett, National Motor Museum, National Rifle Assoc., Mrs R. Peacock, Mrs J. Phillips, C. Powell, S. Purchase, M. Rich, Mrs M. Roe, Mrs S. Rowe, E. Short, Mrs D. Smith, Mrs E. Smith, A.W. Smithers, L. Southall, B. Stephens, D. Tapp, Mrs O. Tocock, Mrs J. Vincent, J. Welch, J. Woodman, Mrs O. Woodman and Mrs W. Wooley.

Although there are over 200 photographs in this book I am sure that there are many more tucked away in old cupboards or drawers somewhere in the area. I hope the publication of this volume encourages people to search out their old photographs – who knows, there might even be a third selection! It would be very sad if such items of interest were to be mistakenly consigned to the bin or a bonfire, and so lost forever.

While every effort has been made to establish copyright and permission sought to reproduce material where appropriate, the author and publisher apologise for any omissions, and will be happy to rectify these in any future edition.

LIST OF ILLUSTRATIONS